Dog
Cookies

healthy, allergen-free treat recipes for your dog

Martina Schöps

D0923684

Hubble & Hattie

Contents

Thank you 5

Introduction 6

Foreword 7

Preface 9

Rewarding your dog in the right way 11

Home-made broth recipe 13

Vegetarian cookies 15

Fish and meat biscuits 27

Gluten-free cookies 39

Healthy, tasty herb cookies 57

Agility treats 69

Festive cookies 75

Little nibbles for cosy nights in 89

Index 96

Hubble & Hattie

www.hubbleandhattie.com

The Hubble & Hattie imprint was launched in 2009 and is named in memory of two very special Westies owned by Veloce's proprietors.

Since the first book, many more have been added to the list, all with the same underlying objective: to be of real benefit to the species they cover, at the same time promoting compassion, understanding and co-operation between all animals (including human ones!)

Hubble & Hattie is the home of a range of books that cover all-things animal, produced to the same high quality of content and presentation as our motoring books, and offering the same great value for money.

More titles from Hubble & Hattie

Animal Grief: How animals mourn each other (Alderton)
Cat Speak (Rauth-Widmann)
Clever dog! Life lessons from the world's most successful animal (O'Meara)
Complete Dog Massage Manual, The – Gentle Dog Care (Robertson)
Dieting with my dog (Frezon)
Dog Games – stimulating play to entertain your dog and you (Blenski)
Dog Speak (Blenski)
Emergency First Aid for dogs (Bucksch)
Exercising your puppy: a gentle & natural approach – Gentle Dog Care (Robertson & Pope)
Fun and Games for Cats (Seidl)
Know Your Dog – The guide to a beautiful relationship (Birmelin)
My dog is blind – but lives life to the full! (Horsky)
My dog is deaf – but lives life to the full! (Willms)
My dog has hip dysplasia – but lives life to the full! (Haüsler)
My dog has cruciate ligament injury – but lives life to the full! (Haüsler)
Older Dog, Living with an – Gentle Dog Care (Alderton & Hall)
Smellorama – nose games for dogs (Theby)
Swim to recovery: canine hydrotherapy healing – Gentle Dog Care (Wong)
Waggy Tails & Wheelchairs (Epp)
Walking the dog: motorway walks for drivers & dogs (Rees)
Winston ... the dog who changed my life (Klute)
You and Your Border Terrier – The Essential Guide (Alderton)
You and Your Cockapoo – The Essential Guide (Alderton)

Important note:
Please ensure that these cookies are not used as your dog's sole nutrition. They are only suitable as treats, and the recipes have been specially developed and tested for this book. Please ensure you are aware of any food intolerances/allergies your dog may have before feeding the treats. The author and Veloce Publishing Ltd shall have neither liability nor responsibility with respect to any loss, damage, or injury caused, or alleged to be caused directly or indirectly, by the information contained within this book.

First published in English in April 2011 by Veloce Publishing Limited, Veloce House, Parkway Farm Business Park, Middle Farm Way, Poundbury, Dorchester, Dorset, DT1 3AR, England. Originally published in Fax 01305 250479/e-mail info@hubbleandhattie.com/web www.hubbleandhattie.com
ISBN: 978-1-845843-80-9 UPC: 6-36847-04380-3
Originally published in 2010 by Kynos Verlag, Dr Dieter Fleig, GmbH, Germany.

Thank you

The biggest thanks go to my husband, Jürgen, who was there to give me advice when I was writing this book. His support never waivered, even when I decided to rewrite all the recipes!

I would also like to thank my parents, my stepchildren and my 'big sister' for all their support and patience.

Special thanks go to my photographer, Claudia Pick, her husband, Dirk, and all the canine models who helped to make this book what it is.

Last but not least, I would like to thank Gisela Rau for her reassurance and teamwork.

Introduction

Proper nutrition is just as important for dogs as it is for people; not only should we pay close attention to what we eat every day, we also need to monitor what we feed our companion animals. Luckily for me, as a trained confectioner and pâtissière, I have plenty of nutritional knowledge.

Since treats contribute to a dog's well-being, and are also an excellent way to help train him, I have devised recipes for healthy treats. It seems that, nowadays, more and more dogs suffer from food allergies and intolerances. I have given this subject a lot of thought and decided to dedicate an entire chapter to it. For this book, I took great care to develop recipes which will be suitable for almost every dog.

As a rule, take care with the ingredients when making your treats. Only use natural ingredients, as this will greatly reduce the likelihood of any food allergies and intolerances. My book will give you plenty of ideas about how to bake healthy treats using natural ingredients for your dog.

I hope you have a lot of fun making treats and rewarding your dog with them!

Martina Schöps

Foreword

Nutrition expert Martina Schöps has put together a collection of her recipes in this unique and contemporary book about baking for dogs. There's no doubt that, nowadays, we give more thought to our pets' welfare than ever before. Dogs have an especially important place in our hearts. Although we no longer need dogs as hunting companions, shepherds for our herds, or guard dogs for our homes, we still value their companionship. They are our four-legged friends, our workout partners, and our fitness trainers. We share holiday and leisure plans and, together, we make a great team when attending classes such as Dog Dancing, Flyball or Agility.

Naturally, we only want what's best for our dogs, just as we want that for ourselves. We can help to calm them using the circular movements of TTouch training; we wage war on their fleas and ticks, and never miss an appointment for a vaccination. Should our animals become ill, we will spend whatever is required on physiotherapy for them, or even acupuncture, gold bead implants, Bach flower extracts and Reiki. No wonder, then, that our dogs – just like our cats – are living longer.

On the downside, more and more animals are suffering from the diseases of modern civilisation. Many dogs are overweight, some so seriously that their quality of life – and certainly their life expectancy – is compromised. Some older dogs suffer with poor dental hygiene because owners ignore veterinary advice to clean their dogs' teeth. Yet, there is no need for older dogs and cats to suffer with bad teeth. Along with basic dental hygiene, eating the right foods can make a huge difference to dental health. Martina Schöps' biscuits and cookies are ideal for this purpose, because, firstly, they are sugar-free; secondly, some of them actually improve dental hygiene; and thirdly, the ingredients used will give your dog fresher breath!

Ten or fifteen years ago, there wouldn't have been a market for a cookbook for dogs. Today, happily, it's a different matter. Many dog owners no longer want to feed their companion prepared food from a bag or a tin, and some get a lot of pleasure from cooking and baking for their canine friends.

At Christmas time particularly, I bake as many treats for my dog as I do for the rest of my family. The dog treats smell and taste so good that we have even tried them ourselves – what was left of them, anyway!

If you enjoy baking, can spare the time and effort, and enjoy trying out new recipes, then this is the book for you – and it will bring you and your dog a lot of joy. Hopefully, many of the dogs owned within your circle of friends will also benefit from these recipes, which makes the effort even more worthwhile.

Those who make their own dog treats know exactly what ingredients go into them, and are creating a great, healthy alternative to the chemical-laden products on offer from the pet food industry. This is not only vital for dogs who suffer from food allergies and intolerances but, if you bake the treats yourself, you can ensure that the biscuits are sugar-free and low in calories, and so are also good news for teeth and figure.

An extra bonus is that they will also help to combat boredom, as chew sticks and other nibbles will occupy your dog when he has to stay in the house on his own. It also means he is less likely to chew on shoes or furniture when his humans are not there!

Author Martina Schöps manufactures and sells fine food for dogs and cats. She knows what tastes great for our animals, and also what does them good. With her many original recipes, you, dear reader, will be able to find a great dog treat for every occasion!

Finally, may I express a personal wish, and one that is echoed wholeheartedly by the publisher of this book? Lots of dog lovers go to great lengths to care for their dogs. Your animals enjoy a wonderful life, and even have people who bake them their own cookies! But we should not forget the thousands of dogs who are waiting in rescue centres for their big chance to find their forever home. You could give them this chance, dear reader! If you're thinking about welcoming a dog into your family, please consider a rescue animal – and indulge him with Martina Schöps' recipes.

Bon appetite!

Dr Claudia Ludwig
Presenter of the television programme *Pets that need a home* (WDR Fernsehen)

Preface

Why make treats yourself?

More and more dogs are suffering from allergies and intolerances to certain chemicals, such as artificial preservatives, vitamins, and animal and plant by-products. This book provides you with recipes for biscuits which can easily be made from common household ingredients and foods with a high biological value.

The most important thing about the treats is what they don't contain

If you are going to make treats for your dog, I'd like to ensure that you know exactly which ingredients they are made with.

The ingredients in commercially manufactured treats are often labelled as being from general food groups; eg meat, grains or minerals.

But what does this actually mean? Exactly which grain or mineral does the product contain?

This could cause problems for those whose dog has a grain intolerance, or a wheat allergy, because it's impossible to identify the exact ingredients in the food. Therefore, making the treats yourself (and knowing what goes into them) means that your dog will enjoy them without regret.

For hundreds of years, herbs have been used for medicinal purposes, which is why I use herbs and seeds in my treats as they offer many health benefits.

Fennel, camomile, mint, sage and thyme relax and calm the stomach and bowel, and will also freshen your dog's breath.

Cinnamon has no specific health benefits, but tastes delicious, not just for us but dogs as well.

Amaranthe, buckwheat and millet are gluten-free, so these are ideal for dogs with coeliac disease.

For dog owners whose dogs suffer from coeliac disease, it's extremely difficult to get hold of treats which can be tolerated, which is why I have devoted an entire chapter to this subject.

Dog cookies

Carob, also known as St John's bread, comes from the fruit pods of the carob tree, and has a similar taste to cocoa. It has a natural sweetness, as well as being rich in vitamins A and B, calcium and iron.

Carob is used as a spice to add flavour. Since cocoa contains caffeine and theobromine (which are extremely harmful to dogs), carob is used as an excellent 'chocolate' replacement in dog biscuits.

Rye and spelt flour are a superb alternative to wheat flour. Wheat flour is not used in any of the recipes in this book, nor do I use it in the manufacture of dog treats in my business. Most cases of grain intolerance are due to wheat flour or soy flour. Therefore, my recipes will give you plenty of ideas how to bake without using wheat flour.

Preparation

When you make treats for your dog, use only products you would eat yourself. A good quality product with a high nutritional value will guarantee it will be well received by your dog, and obviate the possibility of any food intolerances. I recommend that you prepare your own seasoning to add to your treats: fresh or dried herbs will add extra taste, and will mean that your dog savours every last bite!

Home-made broth is used in many of the cookies and treats, so the recipe is given here first.

Storage

I recommend storing all cookies and treats in an airtight container.

Always leave to cool before storing in a cool, dry place.

Any treats that are malleable or moist should be stored in the fridge, but allow them to reach room temperature before serving. Dogs do not like cold meals, as their 'prey' is supposed to be at body temperature and does not come from a fridge!

Treat tip

You will find specific storage advice for each product in the recipe section

Rewarding your dog in the right way

Rewards and treats are very important in a dog's life. Rewards show a dog that he has done something right and give him the encouragement that he needs. When used in the right way, rewards can improve the relationship between dog and human. Treats truly are the way to a dog's heart!

Eating is a basic need and a pleasurable experience for a dog, and we can put this to good use in training.

Ensure that the rewards are not hindering the training in any way; for example, they may sometimes be too distracting for your dog, with the result that he will only respond to food rewards. I have not experienced this myself but, if this happens, then your dog is being rewarded in the wrong way. He may well also sniff your pockets to look for his reward after he has done his 'work,' but this is easily remedied.

Using treats to train a dog is only one of many ways to reward him. Seek advice from dog trainers and other owners about the use of treats in training to find the right way to go about it.

Please remember that although you have made delicious treats, using healthy ingredients such as wholegrain flour, fish, meat, etc, these are not calorie-free! Take care to include the treats as part of your dog's daily food allowance to avoid unwanted weight gain.

Dog cookies

Home-made broth

Ingredients:
1 small free-range chicken or 1 large piece of free-range chicken or turkey
1-2 bunches of carrots, leeks, celery and parsley
1.5 litres (50fl oz) water

Method:
Wash the meat well under running water.

Fill a large pan with water, and add the meat and finely chopped vegetables, then lightly cook the mixture for 2 hours.

Leave the mixture to cool overnight in the fridge. The following day, remove any excess fat, decant the mixture, and take the meat off the bone. (Be careful not to leave any small bones in the meat as these could be dangerous for your dog.) The broth can now be frozen in small portions and stored for future use.

The leftover meat can be used for the turkey treats recipe, or served as a meal with cooked rice, for example.

vegetarian cookies

Vegetarian cookies are eminently suitable for dogs who do not require much animal protein and, of course, if they are fed on a vegetarian diet. The recipes in this section are low in calories and usually very well tolerated

Dog cookies

Spelt Sticks

The thyme in these Spelt Sticks is beneficial to the bowel and stomach

Ingredients:
375g (13oz) wholegrain spelt flour
125g (4oz) rolled oats
50g (2oz) butter
60ml (2fl oz) warm milk
120ml (4fl oz) warm water
1 teaspoon of thyme

Baking time: 30 minutes in a pre-heated oven.
Temperature: Fan-assisted oven 160°C, conventional oven 180°C
Makes approximately 490g (17oz) of Spelt Sticks

Preparation:
Place all of the ingredients in a food processor or hand mixer and process into a dough. Wrap the dough in clingfilm and leave for 30 minutes. Roll out the dough to a thickness of approximately 5mm (⅛in) using a rolling pin. Next, use a knife or a pizza cutter to cut out 4 x 10cm ¼ x ⅝in) rectangles from the dough. Use a fork to prick the dough sticks. Place the spelt sticks on a baking tray covered with greaseproof paper, and bake in a pre-heated oven for 30 minutes. Turn off the oven, open the door and leave the Spelt Sticks to harden for one hour.

Dog cookies

Spinach Treats

Ingredients:
160g (6oz) spelt flour
160g (6oz) rye flour
50g (2oz) quark or low-fat cream cheese
100g (4oz) spinach, frozen
50g (2oz) spelt flakes
150ml (5fl oz) broth or water

Baking time: 30 minutes in a pre-heated oven
Temperature: Fan-assisted oven 160ºC, conventional oven 180ºC
Makes approximately 350g (12oz) of Spinach Treats

Preparation:
Thaw the spinach and squeeze out the excess water. Chop the spinach very finely, using a food processor or a blender.

Place the spelt flour, rye flakes and spelt flakes in a food processor or bowl. Add the spinach, ricotta and broth or water, and process into a smooth dough.

If the dough is too soft, add some wholegrain spelt and work it into the mixture. Wrap the dough in clingfilm and leave for 30 minutes.

Roll out to a thickness of approx 5mm (⅕in), cut into diamond shapes, and prick each biscuit with a fork several times. Place the biscuits on a baking tray covered with greaseproof paper and bake for 30 minutes. Turn off the oven and open the door slightly. Leave for about an hour to allow the biscuits to harden.

Oat and Nut Cookies

Ingredients:
100g (4oz) ground nuts, eg hazelnuts
100g (4oz) rolled oats
250g (9oz) wholegrain spelt flour
50g (2oz) butter or margarine
200ml (7fl oz) water
A pinch of cinnamon
Whole almonds to decorate
1 free-range egg

Baking time: 30 minutes in a pre-heated oven
Temperature: Fan-assisted oven 160°C, conventional oven 180°C
Makes approximately 510g (18oz) of Oat and Nut Cookies

Preparation:
Put the rolled oats, wholegrain spelt, butter, water, and cinnamon in a food processor or hand mixer, and process the mixture into a dough. Wrap the dough in clingfilm and leave for 30 minutes. Then, use a rolling pin to roll out the dough to a thickness of approximately 5mm (⅕in). Cut circles out of the dough to form cookies. Place these on a baking tray covered with greaseproof paper, and use a fork to prick holes in them. Whisk the egg with 3 tablespoons of water, and use a pastry brush to coat the cookies with this mixture. Place 3 almonds on each cookie and press firmly. Bake in a pre-heated oven for 30 minutes. Turn off the oven, open the door, and leave the cookies to harden for one hour.

Rye Crispbreads

Ingredients:
400g (14oz) dark rye flour
100g (4oz) rolled oats
50g (2oz) linseed
300ml (10fl oz) warm milk
50g (2oz) butter or margarine

Baking time: 30 minutes in a pre-heated oven
Temperature: Fan-assisted oven 160°C, conventional oven 180°C
Makes approximately 520g (18oz) Rye Crispbreads

Preparation:
Mix the flour, oats and linseed in a bowl. Melt the butter into the warm milk. Place the flour mixture in a food processor, or hand mixer, and process into a dough. Wrap the dough in clingfilm and leave for 30 minutes. Use a rolling pin to roll out the dough to a thickness of approximately 4mm (⅛in. Use a pizza cutter or knife to make rhombus shapes from the dough. Prick holes in the biscuits with a fork. Put the Rye Crispbreads on a baking tray covered with greaseproof paper and cook for 30 minutes. Turn off the oven and open the oven door slightly to allow the crispbreads to harden for about an hour.

Dog cookies

Banana Biscuits

Ingredients:
1 very ripe banana
250g (9oz) rye flour
150g (5oz) buckwheat flour
1-2 free-range eggs, depending on size
50g (2oz) butter
200ml (7fl oz) warm water
A pinch of carob

Baking time: 40 minutes in a pre-heated oven
Temperature: Fan-assisted oven 150°C, conventional oven 170°C
Makes approximately 450g (16oz) Banana Biscuits

Preparation:
Use a fork to mash the banana to a fine pulp. Place the rye flour, buckwheat flour, banana, eggs, butter, carob and water in a food processor, or use an electric whisk to beat the mixture into a dough. Make sure the dough is not too thick: add some more water, if necessary.

Wrap the dough in clingfilm and leave for 30 minutes. Next, roll the dough into a sausage shape and cut into slices. Mould each into a banana shape and place on a baking tray covered with greaseproof paper.

Bake for 40 minutes in a pre-heated oven. Turn off the oven and open the door slightly to allow the biscuits to harden for about an hour.

carob
carob, also known as St John's bread, is derived from the fruit pods of the carob tree, and has a similar taste to cocoa. Because it does not contain caffeine or theobromine, it is not harmful to dogs, but should not be used in excessive amounts, nevertheless.
You can buy carob from most health food stores.

Dog cookies

Fish & meat biscuits

Dogs love meat and fish, so it makes sense to use these ingredients in your cookies. Your dog will not be able to resist them!

Beef Treats

Hearty, savoury, tasty and a lot of fun to nibble on!

Ingredients:
150g (5oz) minced beef
1 free-range egg
350g (12oz) rye flour
50g (2oz) rolled oats
50ml (2fl oz) rapeseed oil or thistle oil
140ml (5fl oz) water or broth (see page 13 for recipe)

Baking time: 45 minutes in a pre-heated oven
Temperature: Fan-assisted oven 150ºC, conventional oven 170ºC
Makes approximately 470g (17oz) of Beef Treats

Preparation:
Place all of the ingredients in a food processor or hand mixer, and process into a dough. Wrap the dough in clingfilm and leave for 30 minutes.

Roll out the dough to a thickness of about 5mm (⅛in) and cut into bone shapes (or any shape you like). Place on a baking tray covered with greaseproof paper, prick holes in each with a fork, and bake in a pre-heated oven for 45 minutes. Turn off the oven, open the door and leave the biscuits to cool for one hour.

Fish Feasts

Ingredients:
250g (9oz) wholegrain spelt flour
100g (4oz) potato flour
100g (4oz) fish
50ml (2fl oz) broth or water
A pinch of dried parsley
1 free-range egg

Baking time: 30 minutes in a pre-heated oven
Temperature: Fan-assisted oven 160ºC, conventional oven 180ºC
Makes approximately 350g (12oz) of Fish Feasts

Preparation:
Any type of fish can be used for this recipe, so use whichever your dog likes best.

Caution: Ensure all of the bones are removed from the fish.

Use a food processor or immersion blender to shred the fish into very small pieces. You can also use tinned tuna (preferably in brine rather than oil) for this recipe.

Mix the pureed fish with the wholegrain spelt flour, potato flour, broth and parsley, and work into a smooth dough. Wrap the dough in clingfilm and leave for 30 minutes.

Roll out the dough to a thickness of 3mm (⅒in), and cut into small heart shapes, or any shape you like.

Cover a baking tray with greaseproof paper and place the hearts on the tray. Use a fork to prick holes in them.

Bake in a pre-heated oven for 30 minutes, then turn off the oven, open the door and leave the biscuits to cool for one hour.

Treat tip

Regardless of which fish you use, these biscuits should not be stored for too long. Salmon, for example, is quite high in fat, so there is a risk it may go rancid. Store the biscuits in an airtight container, and do not keep them for any longer than two weeks

Turkey-ball Treats

Ingredients:
200g (7oz) wholegrain spelt flour
100g (4oz) rye flour
50g (2oz) buckwheat flour
100g (4oz) turkey breast
1 free-range egg
120ml (4fl oz) broth (see page 13 for recipe) or water
A pinch of herbs, eg Provençal herbs or any other herb mix without salt

Baking time: 45 minutes in a pre-heated oven
Temperature: Fan-assisted oven 150°C, conventional oven 170°C
Makes approximately 370g (13oz) of Turkey-ball Treats

Preparation:
Wash the turkey meat and pat dry. Cube the meat and puree in a food processor.

Add the other ingredients and beat the mixture into a dough. Wrap the dough in clingfilm and leave for 30 minutes.

Knead the dough by hand for a few minutes and then roll into a sausage shape. Using a knife, cut into slices and form little balls from each slice. Cover a baking tray with greaseproof paper and place the turkey-balls on the tray. Make sure that they have room to expand on the tray.

Bake for around 45 minutes. After this time, use a cooking probe to check that the balls are cooked.

If still too gooey in the middle, cook for a further 10 minutes (total cooking time will depend on the size of the turkey-balls).

Turn off the oven, open the door and leave the turkey-balls to cool for one hour.

Ostrich Biscuits with Beetroot

Ostrich meat is very low in fat and is especially suitable for allergy sufferers

Ingredients:
100g (4oz) ostrich meat
200g (7oz) rye flour
100g (4oz) buckwheat flour
50g (2oz) butter or margarine
150ml (5fl oz) beetroot juice
Sesame seeds

Baking time: 30 minutes in a pre-heated oven
Temperature: Fan-assisted oven 160°C, conventional oven 180°C
Makes approximately 330g (12oz) Ostrich Biscuits with Beetroot

Preparation:
Wash the ostrich meat and pat dry. Cut into small pieces and puree in a food processor.

Add the butter, rye flour, buckwheat flour and beetroot juice to the ostrich meat and process the mixture into a dough.

Wrap the dough in clingfilm and leave for 30 minutes.

Roll the dough out to a thickness of 5mm (⅛in) and cut shapes from it to make the biscuits. Use a fork to prick the biscuits, then place them on a baking tray covered with greaseproof paper.

Brush the surface of the biscuits with water and sprinkle with sesame seeds.

Bake in a pre-heated oven for 30 minutes; turn off the oven, open the door and leave the biscuits to cool for one hour.

Beef Jerky

Making beef jerky is laborious and time-consuming, but is worth the effort, particularly if your dog suffers from allergies

Ingredients:
1kg (35oz) meat such as beef, although you can use various types of meat or offal.

Baking time: 5-6 hours in a pre-heated oven
Temperature: Fan-assisted oven 160°C/90°C

Preparation:
Wash the meat, absorb any excess water with kitchen towel and cut off the fat. Cut the meat into very thin slices, no thicker than 5mm (⅛in), and place

on a baking tray covered with greaseproof paper. Bake for one hour in the oven at 160°C, then reduce the heat to 90°C. Dry out the strips of meat for 4-5 hours at this temperature, turning over every 30 minutes.

The drying time can vary – it depends on the type of meat and thickness of the slices. The beef jerky is ready if it is completely dry all the way through. Tripe is well suited as jerky meat and is well-tolerated by dogs, though does have a very unpleasant odour when cooking.

Treat tip

Store the jerky in a cool, dry place. It will last for 6 months as long as no moisture gets to it. If the jerky gets damp, there's a risk it will go mouldy.

Gluten-free cookies
and cookies for allergy sufferers

These are especially suitable for dogs with food allergies, and also those who are sensitive to certain types of food

Dog cookies

Maize and Rice Crackers

Gluten-free

Ingredients:
225g (8fl oz) maize flour
125g (4oz) rice flour
125g (4oz) chicken, eg breast fillet
50ml (2fl oz) rapeseed oil or thistle oil
125ml (4fl oz) broth (see page 13 for recipe) or water

Treat tip

If your dog has an intolerance to chicken, you can use any other type of meat or fish. The most important thing is to ensure that the meat or fish does not have bones in it, and is properly pureed or minced

Baking time: 30-40 minutes in a pre-heated oven
Temperature: Fan-assisted oven 160°C, conventional oven 180°C
Makes approximately 400g (14oz) of Maize and Rice Crackers

Preparation:
Wash the boneless chicken and pat dry. Cut into small cubes and puree in a food processor.

Combine the maize flour, rice flour, meat, oil and broth in the food processor or handmixer and process the mixture into a dough. Wrap the dough in clingfilm and leave for 30 minutes.

Carefully roll the dough to a thickness of 4mm (⅙in) and cut into 3x3cm (1¼x1¼in) squares. This is not as easy as with the dough used in previous recipes because it is gluten-free, and so not sticky (gluten gives dough its 'sticky' quality).

If you have difficulty rolling out the dough, simply form it into pea-sized balls. Cover a baking tray with greaseproof paper and place the little balls or biscuits on the tray.

Bake in a pre-heated oven for 30 minutes, then turn off the oven, open the door and leave the biscuits to cool for one hour.

Dog cookies

Millet Biscuits

Gluten-free

Ingredients:
150g (5oz) wholegrain millet
100g (4oz) potato flour
150g (5oz) tuna in oil
A pinch of dried parsley
1 free-range egg
50ml (2fl oz) broth (see page 13 for recipe) or water
Sesame seeds

Baking time: 40 minutes in a pre-heated oven
Temperature: Fan-assisted oven 160ºC, conventional oven 180ºC
Makes approximately 330g (12oz) of Millet Biscuits

Preparation:
Place the wholegrain millet, potato flour, tuna (with oil), parsley, egg and broth in a food processor or hand mixer and process the mixture into a dough.

Because there's no gluten, the dough will be quite crumbly, so, with moist hands, gently roll the dough into little balls and sprinkle with sesame seeds. Cover a tray with greaseproof paper and lay the balls on the tray. Bake in a pre-heated oven for around 40 minutes. If the biscuits are still a little moist after this time, bake for a further 10 minutes. Turn off the oven, open the door and leave the biscuits inside to cool for one hour.

Amaranth waffles

Gluten-free
Easy and quick to make – every dog is guaranteed to love them!

Ingredients:
50g (2oz) soft butter or margarine
1 free-range egg
200g (7oz) amaranth flour
250ml (8fl oz) carrot juice
20g (1oz) hazelnuts (if your dog has a nut allergy, you could use rolled oats, millet flakes or spelt flake instead)
10g (½oz) baking powder

A pre-heated waffle maker
Makes 5 waffles

Preparation:
Place the butter in the food processor or hand mixer and beat vigourously until it is fluffy. Add the egg. Mix together the flour, nuts or rolled oats and the baking powder, and pour the carrot juice into the butter and egg mixture. Combine all of the ingredients. The dough should be a thick mixture which glides off the spoon. If it's too solid, add more carrot juice; if too runny, add more amaranth flour.

    Spoon three tablespoons of dough into the waffle maker for each waffle.

    Important: Always allow the waffles to cool before eating.

Treat tip

The butter and egg mixture will not really bind properly, but instead will 'collect' together. This is because there's no sugar in the dough. once you add all the other ingredients, the mixture will bind together

Buckwheat Nibbles

Gluten-free

Ingredients:
1 very ripe banana
300g (11oz) buckwheat flour
1 teaspoon carob
100ml (4fl oz) milk or water
1 free-range egg

Baking time: 40 minutes in a pre-heated oven
Temperature: Fan-assisted oven 160ºC, conventional oven 180ºC
Makes approximately 300g (11oz) of Buckwheat Nibbles

Preparation:
Use a fork to mash the banana into a puree. Mix all the other ingredients with the banana and work the mixture into a smooth dough.
Use two teaspoons to form the dough into small round shapes. Line the baking tray with greaseproof paper and place the dough shapes on the tray. Bake for approximately 40 minutes in a pre-heated oven. If, after this time, the Nibbles are not quite done, bake for a further 10 minutes or until completely cooked in the middle. Turn off the oven, leave the door ajar and let the Buckwheat Nibbles harden for an hour.

Spelt Potato Hearts

Ingredients:
300g (11oz) wholegrain spelt flour
150g (5oz) potato flour
100g (4oz) minced beef
50ml (2fl oz) rapeseed oil or thistle oil
200ml (7fl oz) broth (see page 13 for recipe) or water

Baking time: 30 minutes in a pre-heated oven
Temperature: Fan-assisted oven 160°C, conventional oven 180°C
Makes approximately 470g (17oz) Spelt Potato Hearts

Preparation:
Place all of the ingredients together in a food processor or in a bowl.
Process into a smooth dough or, if in a bowl, use an electric whisk with
dough hooks to achieve the same result. Wrap the dough in clingfilm and
leave for 30 minutes.

Roll out the dough to a thickness of approximately 4mm (⅛in) and cut
out small hearts. Use a fork to prick several holes in each biscuit. Cover a

baking tray with greaseproof paper and place
the hearts on the tray. Bake for 30 minutes in a
pre-heated oven. Turn off the oven, leave the
door ajar and let the Spelt Potato Hearts harden
for an hour.

Liver Pretzels

Gluten-free

Ingredients:
300g (11oz) buckwheat flour
250g (9oz) turkey or goose liver
1 free-range egg

Baking time: 45 minutes in a pre-heated oven
Temperature: Fan-assisted oven 160°C, conventional oven 180°C
Makes approximately 420g (15oz) of Liver Pretzels

Preparation:
Wash and then finely puree the liver. Place the liver, buckwheat flour and egg in a food processor or a hand mixer with dough hooks and process into a dough. If the dough is a little sticky, add a small amount of extra buckwheat flour.

Separate the dough into pieces of approximately 30g (1oz) and mould into pretzels. Cover a baking tray with greaseproof paper, place the pretzels on the tray and bake for 45 minutes in a pre-heated oven. Turn off the oven, leave the door ajar and allow the pretzels to harden for an hour.

Chicken Plaits

Gluten-free

Ingredients:
350g (12oz) buckwheat flour
100g (4oz) potato flour
200g (7oz) chicken breast
140ml (5fl oz) carrot juice

Baking time: 50-60 minutes in a pre-heated oven
Temperature: Fan-assisted oven 160°C, conventional oven 180°C
Makes approximately 600g (21oz) of Chicken Plaits

Preparation:
Wash and finely puree the chicken breast, then place this and the rest of the ingredients in a food processor or a hand mixer with dough hooks and process into a dough. If the dough is too sticky, add a little more buckwheat flour.

Weigh out 50g (2oz) pieces of dough. Divide each into three lengths and plait them. Cover a baking tray with greaseproof paper and place the plaits on it. Bake for 50-60 minutes in a pre-heated oven. Turn off the oven, leave the door ajar, and allow the Chicken Plaits to harden for an hour.

Meatloaf

Gluten-free

Ingredients:
500g (18oz) minced beef or minced poultry
100g (4oz) turkey liver
1 free-range egg
½ teaspoon marjoram

Aluminium bread tin
Baking time: 60 minutes in a pre-heated oven
Temperature: Fan-assisted oven 160°C, conventional oven 180°C

Preparation:
Wash and finely puree the turkey liver. Place the mincemeat, egg and marjoram in a bowl and knead vigorously by hand until the mixture is fine and smooth. Add the liver and transfer the mixture into the bread tin. Bake in a pre-heated oven for 60 minutes. Wait for the meatloaf to cool. Tip out of the tin and cut into slices. Then cut the slices into small, bite-size chunks.

Treat tip

The meatloaf will keep in the fridge for 2–3 days. It will also keep very well in the freezer

Healthy, tasty herb cookies

It's the fine herbs which give these cookies their hearty aroma and a delicious taste that your dog will love.
Cookies with camomile, sage, thyme and fennel settle the stomach and bowel, and are especially recommended for dogs with food sensitivities. Ensure you buy only high quality herbs from healthfood or wholefood shops, or perhaps you could even grow the herbs yourself

Dog cookies

Camomile Cookies

Ingredients:
150g (5oz) wholegrain spelt flour
150g (5oz) rye flour
150g (5oz) maize flour
2 tablespoons dried camomile
50ml (2fl oz) rapeseed oil or thistle oil
250ml (8fl oz) broth (see page 13 for recipe) or water

Baking time: 30 minutes in a pre-heated oven
Temperature: Fan-assisted oven 160°C, conventional oven 180°C
Makes approximately 430g (15oz) of Camomile Cookies

Preparation:
Place all the ingredients in a food processor, or a hand mixer with dough hooks, and process the mixture into a smooth dough. Wrap the dough in clingfilm and leave for 30 minutes.

Roll out the dough to a thickness of approximately 4mm (⅛in) and use a pizza cutter or a knife to cut the dough into little squares of around 2 x 2cm (¾ x ¾in).

Cover a baking tray with greaseproof paper, prick holes in the cookies with a fork, and lay them out on the tray. Bake in a pre-heated oven for 30 minutes. Turn off the oven, leave the door ajar and allow the cookies to harden for an hour.

Sage Cookies

Ingredients:
250g (9oz) wholegrain spelt flour
100g (4oz) buckwheat flour
1 teaspoon dried sage
100ml (4fl oz) milk
100ml (4fl oz) water
50g (2oz) cheese, either Gouda or Emmenthal

Baking time: 30 minutes in a pre-heated oven
Temperature: Fan-assisted oven 160°C, conventional oven 180°C
Makes approximately 350g (12oz) of Sage Cookies

Preparation:
Finely grate the cheese and mix together with the rest of the ingredients
in a food processor or a hand whisk with dough hooks. Process the mixture
into a smooth dough. Wrap the dough in clingfilm and leave for 30 minutes,
then roll out to a thickness of approximately 3mm (⅛in) and cut into long
strips roughly 2cm wide x 10cm long (¹⁄₁₀ x 4in). Use a fork to prick holes in
the cookies and lay them on a baking tray which has been covered with
greaseproof paper. Bake for 30 minutes in a pre-heated oven. Allow the
cookies to harden for an hour in the oven with the door slightly ajar.

Thyme Cookies

These cookies are very soft and crumbly, but due to their high butter content, they are also quite high in calories

Ingredients:
125g (4oz) soft butter or margarine
1 free-range egg
150g (5oz) wholegrain spelt flour
1 teaspoon of thyme
A small amount of milk

Baking time: 15-20 minutes in a pre-heated oven
Temperature: Fan-assisted oven 160°C, conventional oven 180°C
Makes approximately 240g (8oz) of Thyme Cookies

Preparation:
Beat the butter in a food processor or with a hand whisk until it is fluffy. Stir in the egg, and then the flour and thyme. The dough should have a liquid consistency. If it is too firm, add a little milk.

   Using a piping bag, pipe small amounts of the mixture onto a baking tray (two tablespoons can be used to form small balls if you do not have a piping bag).

   Bake the cookies in a pre-heated oven for 15-20 minutes. Due to the high butter content, these biscuits will bubble slightly when cooking.

Treat tip

Caution: Ensure that the cookies are not too big and, most importantly, do not feed your dog too many because they are very high in calories. These cookies will keep for up to a maximum of 14 days

Dog cookies

Fennel Cookies

Ingredients:
250g (8oz) rice flour
270g (9oz) rye flour
50g (2oz) wholegrain spelt flakes
300ml (10fl oz) milk
2 free-range eggs
1-2 teaspoons of ground fennel seeds

Baking time: 30 minutes in a pre-heated oven
Temperature: Fan-assisted oven 160°C, conventional oven 180°C
Makes approximately 420g (15oz) Fennel Cookies

Preparation:
Place all of the ingredients in a food processor or hand mixer with dough hooks and process into a smooth dough. Wrap the dough in clingfilm and leave for 30 minutes.

After rolling out to a thickness of approximately 3mm (1/10in), cut shapes out of the dough and prick with a fork. Cover a baking tray with greaseproof paper, put the cookies on the tray and bake in a pre-heated oven for 30 minutes, then allow the cookies to harden for an hour in the oven with the door slightly ajar.

Mint Cookies

These will ensure your dog has fresh breath!

Ingredients:
350g (12oz) wholegrain spelt flour
1 free-range egg
50ml (2fl oz) rapeseed oil or thistle oil
25g (1oz) dried parsley
10g (½oz) dried mint
200ml (7fl oz) milk

Baking time: 30 minutes in a pre-heated oven
Temperature: Fan-assisted oven 160°C, conventional oven 180°C
Makes approximately 380g (13oz) of Mint Cookies

Preparation:
Using a food processor or hand mixer with dough hooks, process all of the ingredients into a smooth dough. Wrap the dough in clingfilm and leave for 30 minutes.

Roll out the dough to a thickness of approximately 3mm (¹⁄₁₀in) and cut shapes of your choice from the dough. Prick holes in the cookies using a fork and place them on a baking tray, covered with greaseproof paper. Bake in a pre-heated oven for 30 minutes. Allow the cookies to harden for an hour in the turned off oven with the door slightly ajar.

Agility treats

Playing, being active and having fun are very important for every dog, and in this chapter you'll find recipes to suit every occasion. These soft, small nibbles are ideal for training, too.

Because of the high moisture content of these treats, they cannot be stored in the fridge for longer than 2-3 days, but they will be fine if stored in the freezer

Agility treats with Beef

Soft nibbles for training, ideal for playing, being active and having fun

Ingredients:
200g (7oz) beef
200g (7oz) beef liver
200g (7oz) rolled oats
200g (7oz) wholegrain spelt flour
3-4 free-range eggs

Baking time: 20-30 minutes in a pre-heated oven
Temperature: Fan-assisted oven 160ºC, conventional oven 180ºC
Makes approximately 780g (28oz) Beef Agility Treats

Preparation:
Wash the beef and the liver, pat dry with kitchen towel and cut into small pieces. Use a food processor to mince the meat. Add the eggs, oats and wholegrain spelt flour and process the mixture on the highest setting for 3 minutes. Cover a deep baking tray with greaseproof paper and smear the paper with butter or margarine. Pour the mixture into the tray to the depth of a finger's width. A little parsley or garlic salt sprinkled on at this stage will add to the flavour, but use the garlic sparingly because your dog's nose is a lot more sensitive than yours! Do not use fresh garlic because it contains a lot of essential oils which can be harmful to dogs. Bake in a pre-heated oven for around 20-30 minutes. Leave to cool and then carefully ease out of the baking tray. When completely cooled, cut into little squares of about 1x1cm (⅜x⅜in).

Agility treats with Poultry Liver (chicken/duck/turkey)

Ingredients:
400g (14oz) poultry liver
200g (7oz) rolled oats
200g (7oz) wholegrain spelt flour
3-4 free-range eggs

Baking time: 20-30 minutes in a pre-heated oven
Temperature: Fan-assisted oven 160ºC, conventional oven 180ºC
Makes approximately 780g (28oz) Poultry Liver Agility Treats

Preparation:
Wash the liver, pat dry with kitchen towel and cut into small pieces. Use a food processor to mince the meat. Add the eggs, oats and wholegrain spelt flour and process the mixture on the highest setting for 3 minutes. Cover a deep baking tray with greaseproof paper, and smear the paper with butter or margarine. Pour the mixture into the tray to the depth of a finger's width. A little parsley or garlic salt sprinkled on at this stage will add to the flavour, but use the garlic sparingly because your dog's nose is a lot more sensitive than yours! Do not use fresh garlic because it contains a lot of essential oils which can be harmful to dogs. Bake in a pre-heated oven for around 20-30 minutes. Leave to cool and then carefully ease out of the baking tray. When completely cooled, cut into little squares of about 1x1cm (⅜x⅜in).

Agility treats with chicken

Ingredients:
300g (11oz) chicken breast fillet
100g (4oz) chicken liver
200g (7oz) rolled oats
200g (7oz) wholegrain spelt flour
3-4 free-range eggs

Baking time: 20-30 minutes in a pre-heated oven
Temperature: Fan-assisted oven 160°C, conventional oven 180°C
Makes approximately 780g (28oz) Chicken Agility Treats

Preparation:
Wash the chicken and the liver, pat dry with kitchen roll and cut into small pieces. Use a food processor to mince the meat. Add the eggs, oats and wholegrain spelt flour and process the mixture on the highest setting for 3 minutes. Cover a deep baking tray with greaseproof paper and smear the paper with butter or margarine. Pour the mixture into the tray to the depth of a finger's width. A little parsley or garlic salt sprinkled on at this stage will add to the flavour, but use the garlic sparingly because your dog's nose is a lot more sensitive than yours! Do not use fresh garlic because it contains a lot of essential oils which can be harmful to dogs. Bake in a pre-heated oven for around 20-30 minutes. Leave to cool and then carefully ease out of the baking tray. When completely cooled, cut into little squares of about 1x1cm (⅜x⅜in).

Festive cookies

There are plenty of festive days that we celebrate each year, and, even in a dog's life, there are many special occasions for him to enjoy. How about a slice of birthday cake, or some Easter biscuits hidden in the garden for him to find? Or maybe some delicious cookies to celebrate her first day at dog-school? There are lots of reasons to celebrate with your dog, and here are some scrumptious recipes for those special occasions

Easter Biscuits with Carrots

Ingredients:
150g (5oz) rye flour
150g (5oz) wholegrain spelt flour
150g (5oz) potato flour
150g (5oz) carrots
50ml (2fl oz) rapeseed oil or thistle oil
170ml (6fl oz) broth (see page 13 for recipe) or water

Baking time: 35 minutes in a pre-heated oven
Temperature: Fan-assisted oven 160°C, conventional oven 180°C
Makes approximately 430g (15oz) Easter Biscuits

Preparation:
Wash the carrots, peel and finely grate them. Combine the carrot gratings and the other ingredients in a food processor or hand mixer with dough hooks and process into a smooth dough. Wrap the dough in clingfilm and leave for 30 minutes.

    Roll out the dough to a thickness of approximately 4mm (⅛in) and cut different shapes from the dough, such as Easter bunnies or chicks.

    Cover a baking tray with greaseproof paper, prick the cookies several times with a fork and place them on the baking tray. Bake in a pre-heated oven for around 35 minutes. Turn off the oven, leave the door slightly ajar and allow the cookies to cool for 1 hour.

Treat tip
These cookies can be beautifully packaged to make an ideal Easter present!

Dog cookies

Christmas Cookies

Your dog will not be able to resist the enticing smell of these cinnamon cookies!

Ingredients:
350g (12oz) wholegrain spelt flour
100g (4oz) rolled oats
50g (2oz) soft butter or margarine
100ml (4fl oz) milk
75ml (3fl oz) water
1 free-range egg
A pinch of cinnamon

Baking time: 30 minutes in a pre-heated oven
Temperature: Fan-assisted oven 160°C,
conventional oven 180°C
Makes approximately 460g (16oz) of Christmas
Cookies

Preparation:
Place all of the ingredients in a food processor or hand mixer with dough hooks and process into a dough. Wrap the dough in clingfilm and leave for 30 minutes.

Roll the dough to a thickness of around 4mm (³⁄₁₆in) and cut Christmas-themed shapes from it. Cover a baking tray with greaseproof paper, use a fork to prick each cookie several times, and then lay them out on the baking tray. Bake in a pre-heated oven for 30 minutes. Turn off the oven, leave the door slightly ajar and allow the cookies to harden for one hour.

Treat tip

You can also use this recipe to make christmas tree decorations.

Roll out the dough a little thicker (around 5mm/quarter inch) and cut out large shapes, such as christmas trees or stars. Then use a knitting needle to make a hole at the top of the cookie (you can later thread a ribbon through the hole and hang the cookie on the tree). Prick the cookies plenty of times with a fork to prevent bubbles forming in the dough.

Bake in a pre-heated oven for at least 40 minutes; if you're not sure whether the cookies are ready after this time, leave them in for another 10 minutes. Then leave the oven door slightly ajar and allow the cookies to harden for one hour.

Once the cookies are cooled, pull a ribbon through the hole in the top of each and hang them on the christmas tree.

They can also be beautifully packaged to make the perfect christmas present!

Seasonal Cookies

Special cookies for special days. This is a slightly more elaborate, but very tasty recipe

Ingredients:
400g (14oz) wholegrain spelt flour
100g (4oz) buckwheat flour
100g (4oz) cheese, Gouda or Emmenthal
100g (4oz) salmon
100g (4oz) turkey
50g (2oz) soft butter
50g (2oz) spelt flakes
150ml (5fl oz) broth (see page 13 for recipe) or water
Mixed herbs (no salt)
Makes approximately 600g (21oz) of Seasonal Cookies

Baking time: 30 minutes in a pre-heated oven
Temperature: Fan-assisted oven 160°C, conventional oven 180°C

Preparation:
Wash the salmon and liver and pat dry with kitchen towel. Ensure that all bones are removed from the salmon. Cut into small pieces and puree in the food processor. Grate the cheese very finely. Add the liver, salmon and cheese to the rest of the ingredients and, using a food processor or hand mixer with dough hooks, process the mixture into a dough. Wrap the dough in clingfilm and leave for 30 minutes.

Roll out the dough to a thickness of around 3mm (¹⁄₁₀in)and cut out little shapes. Prick the cookies several times with a fork, place them on a baking tray covered with greaseproof paper and bake for 30 minutes in a pre-heated oven. Then turn off the oven, leave the door slightly ajar and allow the cookies to harden for one hour.

Birthday Cake

Celebrate your dog's birthday in style! Make a cake, invite some friends (yours and his), and get the party going. This cake will serve 8-10 dogs, depending on size

Ingredients:
(For a 26cm diameter cake tin)
400g (14oz) wholegrain spelt flour
200g (7oz) turkey or chicken liver
100g (4oz) chicken breast
150g (5oz) rolled oats
5 free-range eggs
250g (9oz) butter
A little carrot juice
20g (½oz) baking powder

Baking time: 40-50 minutes in a pre-heated oven
Temperature: Fan-assisted oven 160°C, conventional oven 180°C

Preparation:
Wash the liver and chicken, pat dry with kitchen roll and finely puree in a food processor.

Beat the butter until it is fluffy and fold in the eggs. Stir in the liver and chicken. Then mix in the flour and baking powder and, finally, stir in the carrot juice.

The mixture should have a slightly liquid consistency. If too runny, add some more flour; if too firm then thin with either milk or carrot juice.

Grease the cake tin well, pour in the dough and smooth flat.

Bake for 40-50 minutes in a pre-heated oven. After 40 minutes, prick the cake with a toothpick (or a knife) to see if it is done. Insert the knife into the middle of the cake, and if it comes out clean with no dough on it, then the cake is ready. If there's dough on the knife, bake for another 10 minutes and repeat the test process.

After the cake has cooled, it can be decorated with some of the other cookies and treats in this book, such as Turkey Balls, Spelt Potato Hearts, Banana Biscuits or Cream Cheese. There are no limits so let your imagination run away with you! You can also use Cream Cheese as 'cement' to ensure the decorations stay put.

Treat tip

The cake can be stored in the fridge for 2–3 days, but ensure it's at room temperature before serving.

Dog cookies

Coconut Muffins

Ingredients:
150g (5oz) butter or margarine
3 free-range eggs
100g (4oz) coconut flakes
400g (14oz) wholegrain spelt flour
1 packet of baking powder
150-200ml (5-7fl oz) carrot juice or milk
12 cake papers

Treat tip

The muffins can be stored at room temperature for around 2–3 days, but you can freeze them if you need to keep them any longer than this

Baking time: 45 minutes in a pre-heated oven
Temperature: Fan-assisted oven 150°C, conventional oven 170°C
Makes approximately 12 Coconut Muffins

Preparation:
Beat the butter and eggs until they are fluffy, then stir in the coconut flakes. Mix the flour with the baking powder and sieve. Fold the carrot juice or milk into the dough until the dough has a slightly runny consistency.

Fill each cake paper with the mixture until two-thirds full and bake in a pre-heated oven for 45 minutes. Use a knife to check if the muffins are completely cooked, as with the birthday cake. If the knife comes out clean, the muffins are cooked, but if there's dough on the knife, then bake the muffins for a further 10 minutes, repeating the test process after this time to check that the muffins are cooked through.

Little nibbles for cosy nights in

When it's cold and wet outside, what could be nicer than a cosy evening in? Or how about spending a beautiful summer's evening relaxing in the garden? Some tasty nibbles are the perfect accompaniment – here are a few ideas for some you can make

Fruit & vegetable Crisps

Ingredients:
A selection of vegetables such as carrots, celery, parsnips
A selection of fruits such as apples and bananas

Drying time: 6-8 hours
Temperature: 60°C in a convection oven

Preparation:
Wash and dry the fruit and vegetables and cut into slices of 3mm ⅒in). Lay the slices on a baking tray covered with greaseproof paper and dry them out in a pre-heated oven for around 6-8 hours. The oven door should be left slightly ajar whilst the fruit and vegetables are drying to allow the moisture to escape more easily.

The chips are ready once they are completely dry. If any moisture remains, they could go mouldy. The drying out time varies hugely and depends on the moisture content of the fruit and vegetables and the thickness of the slices.

Store the chips in an airtight container in a cool, dry place. They will keep for 3 months as long as they have been dried out thoroughly.

Popcorn

Fun for every dog party!

Ingredients:
Popcorn maize
1 tablespoon of rapeseed oil or sunflower oil

Preparation:
Lightly heat the oil in a large, deep pan and add 50g of popcorn.

Put a lid on the pan. At a medium heat, after a short time the corn will begin to pop. Wait until you cannot hear any more popping sounds. Lay the popcorn on a kitchen towel, leave to cool and then serve.

The popcorn will keep for 5 days in a cool, dry place.

Doggie Ice Cream

Refreshment for hot summer days!
Pop a few into your dog's Kong® to
keep him cool and absorbed

Ingredients:
1 natural yoghurt
1 ripe banana
Mixed herbs

Preparation:
Mash the banana with a fork and then
mix in the yoghurt. Place a sprinkle
of herbs at the bottom of each
compartment in an ice-cube tray and
add enough mixture to bring it level
with the top of the compartment.
Place in the freezer.

Caution!

Don't feed your dog too many of these, because
some dogs do not tolerate cold ice cream very
well

Cream Cheese Pralines

Ingredients:
200g (7oz) cream cheese
100g (4oz) low fat quark
Sesame seeds
Finely chopped parsley
Linseed seeds
Small pieces of raw vegetables
(carrots/broccoli/parsnip)

Preparation:
Mix the cream cheese and quark,
then chop the vegetables into
tiny pieces and add these to the
mixture. Moisten your hands and
make little balls out of the mixture,
then roll them in the sesame seeds,
linseed seeds, parsley or other
herbs.

Treat tip

Beautifully packaged, these treats make
the perfect gift!

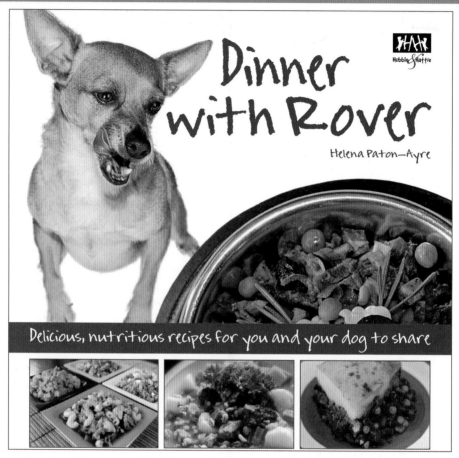

Christiane Blenski

Dog Games

Stimulating play to entertain your dog and you

Hubble & Hattie

Quick and easy-to-get-the-hang-of games, so you spend less time reading and more time playing. These new motivational games have been thoroughly tested by Christiane Blenski, her dog, Jaden, and all their friends. Whether using his body, his brain, or both; just the two of you or with children as well; whether inside or out, here's the definitive and best guide to all the fun, new games that your dog will love!

- Includes a games pace test
- Over 50 new games
- Ideas for all dogs: large, small, young and old
- The motivational book for everyone who wants to have more fun with their dog
- Every game explained in detail and colourfully illustrated with several photos

128 pages • 245 colour pictures • Paperback • 250x250mm • ISBN: 978-1-845843-32-8 • £15.99*/$32.95*

Index

Agility Treats with Beef 71
Agility Treats wth Chicken 73
Agility Treats with Poultry Liver 72
Amaranth Waffles 45

Banana Biscuits 25
Beef Jerky 37
Beef Treats 29
Birthday Cake 83
Buckwheat Nibbles 47

Camomile Cookies 59
Chicken Plaits 53
Christmas Cookies 79
Coconut Muffins 87
Cream Cheese Pralines 93

Doggie Ice Cream 93

Easter Biscuits with Carrots 77

Fennel Cookies 65
Fish Feasts 31
Fruit and Vegetable Crisps 91

Liver Pretzels 51

Maize and Rice Crackers 41
Meatloaf 55
Millet Biscuits 43
Mint Cookies 67

Oat and Nut Cookies 21
Ostrich Biscuits with Beetroot 35

Popcorn 91

Rye Crispbreads 23

Sage Cookies 61
Seasonal Cookies 81
Spelt Potato Hearts 49
Spelt Sticks 17
Spinach Treats 19

Thyme Cookies 63
Turkey-ball Treats 33